D05025961

To DIANE

FRom ....

CONTENTS

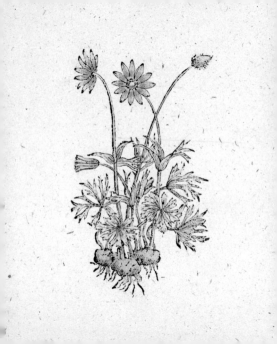

INTRODUCTION

According to the Book of Genesis, the history of humankind began in a garden. And perhaps it is because we were exiled from Eden that we take such pleasure in staking out a plot of earth and cultivating it as our own private creation. It is there, in our gardens, that the changing seasons are most acutely felt, and the subtle pleasures of Nature's enduring cycle most wholly appreciated.

Gathered in this book are quotations, verse, and homey advice on each phase of the gardener's year. Together they comprise a celebration of the most profoundly pure joys known to the human spirit. . . .

The joys of the garden.

BLOSSOMING

Slayer of winter, art thou here
    again?
O welcome, thou that bring'st the
    Summer nigh!

William Morris

Spring has come when you can put your foot on three daisies.

Traditional folk wisdom

Winter lingered so long in the lap of spring that it occasioned a great deal of talk.

Bill Nye

There is life in the ground: It goes into the seeds, and it also, when it is stirred up, goes into the man who stirs it.

Charles Dudley Warner.

The nicest thing about the promise of spring is that sooner or later she'll have to keep it.

Mark Beltaire

SOME SPRING-BLOOMING BULBS

Crocus

DAFFODIL, or *narcissus*

GLORY-OF-THE-SNOW, or *chionodoxa*

HYACINTH, or *hyacinthus*

SNOWDROP, or *galanthus*

TROUT LILY, or *erythronium*

TULIP, or *tulipa*

WINDFLOWER, or *anemone blanda*

SOME SPRING-BLOOMING PERENNIALS

BLUESTAR, or *amsonia*

COLUMBINE, or *aquilegia*

LILY OF THE VALLEY, or *convallaria*

LUPINE, or *lupinus*

PASQUEFLOWER, or *anemone pulsatilla*

PEONY, or *paeonia*

SIBERIAN BUGLOSS, or *brunnera*

SPURGE, or *euphorbia*

I wandered lonely as a cloud
That floats on high o'er vales and
    hills,
When all at once I saw a crowd,
A host of golden daffodils;
Beside the lake, beneath the trees,
Fluttering and dancing in the breeze.

Continuous as the stars that shine
And twinkle on the milky way,
They stretched in never-ending line
Along the margin of the bay:

Ten thousand saw I at a glance,
Tossing their heads in sprightly
    dance.

William Wordsworth

The first day of spring was once the time for taking the young virgins into the fields, there in dalliance to set an example in fertility for Nature to follow. Now we just set the clock an hour ahead and change the oil in the crankcase.

E. B. White

A lily of a day
Is fairer in May,
Although it fall and die that night;
It was a plant and flower of light.
In small proportions we just beauties
    see;
And in short measures, life may
    perfect be.

Ben Jonson

HARDEN, THEN PINCH, YOUR SEEDLINGS

Before transplanting seedlings, place them outdoors for an increasing period of time each day. A week or so of such hardening off will prepare them for the bright sun and more stressful temperatures of the garden. Do not transplant seedlings, however, while nighttime temperatures remain below 50°F. After transplanting, pinch off the tops to promote bushy growth.

SOME SPRING-BLOOMING SHRUBS

BARBERRY, or *berberis*

Forsythia

HONEYSUCKLE, or *lonicera*

LILAC, or *syringa*

Magnolia

MOCK ORANGE, or *philadelphus*

Spirea

PRUNE YOUR SHRUBS EVERY SPRING

Take a look at your shrubs each spring to determine whether they need pruning. Look for branches broken or damaged by stormy winter weather, as well as unsightly stragglers. Cut dead or damaged wood back to healthy, outward-facing shoots. Prune back the stragglers by half—again to healthy, outward-facing shoots.

RIPENING

Pleasures are like poppies spread,
You seize the flow'r, the bloom is
shed.

Robert Burns

DISBUDDING AND DEADHEADING ROSES

To encourage larger blooms in your roses, snip off any buds that appear within six inches of the terminal bud on each stem. Then once the blooms are spent, remove them. This is deadheading, and it often encourages second bloomings later in the season.

Bees are not as busy as we think they are. They just can't buzz any slower.

Kin Hubbard

To own a bit of ground, to scratch it with a hoe, to plant seeds, and watch their renewal of life——this is the commonest delight of the race, the most satisfactory thing a man can do.

Charles Dudley Warner

PINCH YOUR MUMS

To guarantee a full-flowering chrysanthemum, pinch off all the shoots above the topmost full leaves at least ninety days before the plant's blooming time. This encourages additional side shoots and also promotes root development.

SOME SUMMER-BLOOMING PERENNIALS

Astilbe

BABY'S BREATH, or *gypsophilia*

BEE BALM, or *monarda*

BUTTERFLY WEED, or *asclepias*

GLOBE THISTLE, or *echinops*

Phlox

TICKSEED, or *coreopsis*

YARROW, or *achilllea*

What a man needs in gardening is a cast-iron back, with a hinge in it.

Charles Dudley Warner

Water is H_2O, hydrogen two parts, oxygen one, but there is also a third thing, that makes it water and nobody knows what that is.

D. H. Lawrence

Thou art the Iris, fair among the
    fairest,
Who, armed with golden rod
And winged with the celestial azure,
    bearest
The message of some God.

Thou art the Muse, who far from
    crowded cities
Hauntest the sylvan streams,
Playing on pipes of reed the artless
    ditties
That come to us as dreams.

30

O flower-de-luce, bloom on, and let
   the river
Linger to kiss thy feet!
O flower of song, bloom on, and
   make forever
The world more fair and sweet.

Henry Wadsworth Longfellow

WATERING ROSES

In hot midsummer weather, water rosebushes at their crowns because overhead watering may damage the flowers. Before plants come into bloom, however, mist their buds with a fine spray of water. Do this early in the day, though, so the blooms don't mildew overnight.

A plant is like a self-willed man, out of whom we can obtain all which we desire, if we will only treat him his own way.

Goethe

Summer ends, and Autumn comes, and he who would have it otherwise would have high tide always and a full moon every night.

Hal Borland

SOME SUMMER-BLOOMING SHRUBS

Buddleia

CINQUEFOIL, or *potentilla*

Fuchsia

Hibiscus

Hydrangea

MOUNTAIN LAUREL, or *kalmia*

SOME SUMMER-BLOOMING BULBS

Allium

Begonia

Dahlia

Gladiolus

OVERCROWDING

When plants such as daffodils or irises are left undisturbed for a number of years, they tend to become overcrowded, which can eventually lead to a loss of bloom. When that happens, the wise gardener digs up the plants, divides them, and then re-plants. In general, divisions should be performed either before growth begins in the early spring or after it has slowed in the late fall.

HARVESTING

Every leaf speaks bliss to me,
Fluttering from the autumn tree.

Emily Brontë

There is no season when such pleasant and sunny spots may be lighted on, and produce so pleasant an effect on the feelings, as now in October.

Nathaniel Hawthorne

November's sky is chill and drear,
November's leaf is red and sear.

Sir Walter Scott

LIFT YOUR TENDER TUBERS

If your climate includes a snowy winter, dig up your tender tubers and bulbs—such as dahlias, begonias, and gladiolus—in early autumn, about the same time you plant your tulips. Overwinter them in a cool, dry place. Then replant them in the spring once the danger of a frost has passed.

HOW TO BUY BULBS

Healthy bulbs, like healthy garden-ers, are firm, unshriveled, and have no soft spots.

40

HOW TO NATURALIZE BULBS

Some bulbs, such as crocuses and narcissi, often look more attractive naturalized in a lawn or meadow than planted in an ornamental bed. A good way to naturalize these bulbs is to scatter by hand and then plant them where they land.

HOW TO GROUP BULBS IN YOUR LAWN

To group bulbs such as daffodils in your lawn, begin by cutting a figure H in the sod with a knife or, even better, an edger. Peel back the turf, loosen the soil underneath, fertilize with a little bone meal, and plant the bulbs at the correct depth. Then gently roll back the sod, firm the plot, and water thoroughly.

SOME FALL-BLOOMING PERENNIALS

Aster

Chrysanthemum

GOLDENROD, or *solidago*

STONECROP, or *sedum*

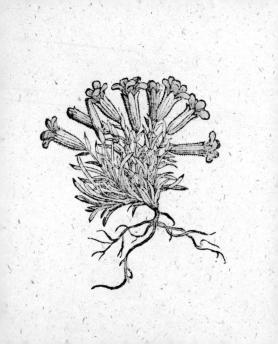

SHRUBS FOR FALL COLOR

BLUEBEARD, or *caryopteris*

Euonymus

FIRE THORN, or *pyracantha*

Fothergilla

The scarlet of the maples can shake
  me like a cry
Of bugles going by.
And my lonely spirit thrills
To see the frosty asters like a smoke
  upon the hills.

Bliss Carman

For man, autumn is a time of harvest,
of gathering together. For nature, it is
a time of sowing, of scattering abroad.

Edwin Way Teale

PREPARE PERENNIALS FOR THE WORST

In cold regions, prune perennials down to the ground, removing the foliage that would otherwise die during the winter. This decreases the risk of rot-induced disease. In very cold regions, cover your least hardy perennials with a layer of evergreen boughs or salt marsh hay. Gradually remove this mulch as the ground thaws in spring.

FREEZING HERBS

You can preserve most fresh, leafy herbs by freezing them. First blanch the leaves by dunking them in boiling water (one pint for every two and a half ounces of herb) for approximately thirty seconds. After blanching the leaves, plunge them into an ice-water bath for one minute. Then remove the leaves and pat dry before packing them into airtight plastic bags. Remember to label each bag before placing it in the freezer.

DRYING HERBS

Harvest herbs early on a dry morning before any buds have opened. For large-leaved herbs, such as mint and basil, strip the healthy leaves from the plant stems and wash them carefully in cold tap water. Then spread them out on a wire screen or newspaper to dry.

For small-leaved herbs—such as rosemary, tarragon, and thyme—gather the stems into small, loose bundles. Then wrap the bundles in muslin and hang them, stems up, from a clothesline in a dry room with a constant temperature of 70°-75°F. The leaves are ready for use when they have dried to a brittle, crumbly state.

WINTERING

Willow whiten, aspens quiver,
Little breezes dusk and shiver.

Alfred, Lord Tennyson

Contrary to general opinion, February is the driest month of the year, and, when the weather is not exceptionally severe, affords a favourable opportunity for pushing on outdoor work of all descriptions.

From The Garden Oracle *(1896)*

Such is a winter eve. Now for a merry fire, some old poet's pages, or else serene philosophy, or even a healthy book of travels to last far into the night, eked out perhaps with the walnuts which we gathered in November.

Henry David Thoreau

SOME PLANTS FOR WINTER INTEREST

Astilbe

BROOM, or *cystius*

DOGWOOD, or *cornus*

HEATH, or *erica*

HEATHER, or *calluna*

HOLLY, or *ilex*

STONECROP, or *sedum*

Viburnum

Few berries on holly branches mean a mild winter, since the birds will have much other food available; abundant holly berries mean a harsh winter with scarce other provisions for birds.

Ancient folk wisdom

SHRUBS THAT FLOWER ON NEW SHOOTS

Summer- and fall flowering shrubs that flower on new shoots—such as bluebeard (caryopteris), buddleia, hydrangea, and crape myrtle (lagerstroemia)—should be pruned in late winter or very early spring to encourage larger blooms. Cut back each of the previous year's shoots to within two or three buds of its base. Do not cut back older wood unless you want to change the shape of the shrub.

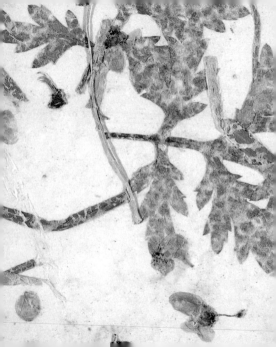

USEFUL ADVICE

TO PREVENT SLUGS FROM
DAMAGING FRUIT TREES

Wrap the trunk of the fruit tree with two or three strands of horsehair so full of shrubs and straggling Points of the Hair that neither a slug nor a snail can pass over them without wounding themselves to Death.

From A Curious Gentleman in Hertfordshire

It is thus with farming: If you do one thing late, you will be late in all your work.

Cato the Elder

Better is a dinner of herbs where love is than a stalled ox and hatred therewith.

Proverbs

AN OLD WIVES' TALE

To discourage moles, stand open bottles about two or three yards apart in the moles' run. The wind whistling in the bottlenecks will scare them away.

PLANT YOUR SHRUB IN A TIDY BED

To look its best, a shrub should be planted in a bed cut neatly out of the lawn. You can use a makeshift compass to outline the bed. First, insert a stake into the lawn at the proposed center of the bed. Then tie a string to the stake, and tie a knife to the string at the proposed radius of the bed. Finally, cut with the knife in a circular motion to mark the bed. Then carefully remove the sod using a spade.

If swallows fly upon the water low,
Or woodlice seem in armies for to
    go;
If flies or gnats or fleas infest a bite,
Or sting more than their wont by
    day and night;
If toads hie home or frogs do croak
    amain,
Or peacocks cry—soon after look
    for rain.

From The New Book of Knowledge
(1758)

NEW PLANTS FROM TIP AND LEAF CUTTINGS

Using a stick, make a few holes in some potting soil. Then insert either a tip or a leaf cutting into the hole. Cover the pot with a clear plastic bag, securing it with a rubber band. Once the cuttings have rooted, transplant them into individual pots.

COMPANION PLANTING OF HERBS

The following aromatic herbs are natural repellents of insect pests, and are therefore valuable companion plants for your garden: mint, parsley, sage, rosemary, and thyme.

These herbs attract bees, which help pollinate other plants: dill, hyssop, lemon balm, thyme.

Radishes pulled up as the moon wanes
will cure corns and warts.

Traditional folk wisdom

If it moves slowly enough, step on it;
if it doesn't, leave it—it'll probably
kill something else.

Traditional wisdom on the control of pests

SOME OLD WIVES' TALES

A sure way to prevent mice from invading your garden is to wash your cat and sprinkle the water over the garden.

Black thread tied around fruit bushes will protect them from birds.

To keep rabbits from invading your garden, plant a row of onions, chives, or garlic around the garden, since rabbits never cross such a border.

GROWING A PINEAPPLE

You can grow an attractive houseplant by potting the leafy top of a pineapple. And by sealing a healthy pineapple plant in a plastic bag along with a ripe apple for about five days, you can even grow pineapples. The decaying apple produces a gas that stimulates the plant to produce fruit.

A RECIPE FOR POTTING SOIL

2   parts garden soil
1   part peat moss or leaf mold
1   part perlite, coarse sand, or bird
    gravel
1/4 part bone meal or 1/8 part
    superphospate
1/2 part composted cow manure

THE
SOUL
OF GARDENING

How cunningly nature hides every wrinkle of her inconceivable antiquity under roses and violets and morning dew!

Ralph Waldo Emerson

Earth laughs in flowers.

Ralph Waldo Emerson

However much you knock at nature's door, she will never answer you in comprehensible words.

Ivan Turgenev

Nature never did betray the heart that loved her.

William Wordsworth

I like trees because they seem more resigned to the way they have to live than other things do.

Willa Cather

Deep in their roots,
All flowers keep the light.

Theodore Roethke

In nature there are neither rewards
nor punishments—there are conse-
quences.

R. G. Ingersoll

Deviation from Nature is deviation
from happiness.

Dr. Johnson

Anyone who has got any pleasure at all
from nature should try to put something back. Life is like a superlative
meal and the world is the maître
d'hôtel. What I am doing is the equiv-
alent of leaving a reasonable tip.

Gerald Durrell

Man is a complex being who makes deserts bloom and lakes die.

Gil Stern

When the oak is felled the whole forest echoes with its fall, but a hundred acorns are sown by an unnoticed breeze.

Thomas Carlyle

Each flower is a soul blossoming out to nature.

Gerard de Nerval

Flowers are the sweetest things God ever made and forgot to put a soul into.

Henry Ward Beecher